THE WEALTHY THINK DIFFERENTLY

HOW TO DISCOVER, AND CHALLENGE YOUR FINANCIAL PHILOSOPHY

Printed in the United States of America.

ISBN: 978-1-63385-258-7

Designed and published by

Word Association Publishers
205 Fifth Avenue
Tarentum, Pennsylvania 15084

www.wordassociation.com
1.800.827.7903

THE **WEALTHY THINK DIFFERENTLY**

HOW TO **DISCOVER, AND CHALLENGE** *YOUR* **FINANCIAL PHILOSOPHY**

JOEL M. JOHNSON, CFP®

IMPORTANT — READ THIS FIRST

This book is my opinion based on my professional and personal observations.

I've observed friends and acquaintances who were wealthy, others who never seemed to get ahead, and still others who were miserable.

The ideas and statements in this book are not absolutes; they do not apply to all who are wealthy or all who are struggling financially.

I am the majority owner in an investment advisory firm registered with the Securities and Exchange Commission as well as the majority owner of an insurance agency.

Nothing in this book is a recommendation of an investment or a promise of future results. This book's goal is to get you thinking about your thinking and behavior around money.

I want this book to help people improve their relationship with their finances. It is clearly not intended to recommend investment products or strategies because as you well know, recommendations need to be customized to the individual's needs.

TABLE OF CONTENTS

INTRODUCTION

To be successful at handling money no matter the amount, you have to realize the importance of how and what you think about money as well as what you want to do with it.

Our team at Johnson Brunetti look at money as a tool that will allow people to achieve freedom, not something to be a slave to, worry about, or to obsess over. None of us can truly consider ourselves free if we are obsessed with anything, and that especially includes money.

Here's a quick test—no right or wrong here, no pass or fail, just answer from your gut. If you were planning a vacation, would your first question be

"Where would I like to go?" or would it be "What can I afford to spend on a vacation?" Most people will end up asking themselves both questions of course, but what I think is so important is which one they ask first. That can speak volumes about their attitudes toward money. Do they look upon it as a restraining or a liberating factor?

In my book *The Money Map*, which I published in 2011 and have updated since, I offered my clients and my readers a simple, one-page plan for retirement and investment success (that's actually the book's subtitle). My idea with that book was to offer some solid advice and strategies I'd come up with during my years as a CFP™ who focused (and still does) on investment and retirement planning.

In it, I cover investing in mutual funds and real estate, avoiding advice from untrustworthy sources, the greed–entitlement–arrogance attitude of Wall Street, income-producing investments, and many other topics of interest to anyone who wants to be careful about his or her money. That covers us all, right? That book is still out there, and its advice is still valuable.

But in this book, I want to do something different; I want to consider the attitudes we have toward money—yours, mine, wealthy people's, everyone's—and what effect our attitudes can have on the financial decisions we make or don't make. Some people approach their financial concerns with confidence while others do so with fear and trepidation. What's the difference between those two points of view? The emotions that money evokes in them.

I've long since learned that the attitudes people have toward their money can be more important than how much money they have. Their attitudes toward wealth will drive them to do this rather than that, to go with their hearts rather than their minds or vice versa. Their attitudes will exert tremendous influence over their financial decisions—what to invest in, how much to invest, what risks they're willing to take in their investments, when they want to retire, when they can retire, on and on.

Our philosophies about money and wealth are critical issues for us today and in the future—for our families today and for our families years down the road. Do we view money as an end in itself—the more the better—or do we look upon it as a tool to help us gain an end we consider more important? Do we feel ashamed if we don't have as much as we'd like to have? Do we feel embarrassed about how much we have? Does wealth bring happiness in itself, or does it allow us to achieve happiness as we individually define it?

I want to encourage you to answer these and many other questions about money, wealth, finances, savings—the whole shebang—for yourself. In doing so, I suspect you'll discover things about yourself you never knew or felt or weren't quite able to verbalize. That knowledge will allow you to identify and foster the attitudes you have that are working in your favor now and those that could be holding you back from achieving freedom—financial and otherwise. I want to boost your confidence and reduce your fear about your financial concerns. I think what you'll learn is that true wealth is an attitude, not a number.

At Johnson Brunetti, our constant focus is on our clients—we strive to give them a sense of security and the feeling of confidence that their money is in good, reliable, and thoughtful hands. We do this by consistently responding to them through phone calls, emails, meetings—whatever it takes. We can offer quick answers to their questions because we have the staff necessary to find the answers in a timely fashion. We want all our clients to reach their financial goals for retirement as well as their other goals—leaving inheritances to their families, benefitting their charities, and their other specific and personal desires.

Yours are worthy goals. Let's get started achieving them.

CHAPTER 1

THE RELATIONSHIPS OF THE WEALTHY

Let me tell you about the very rich. They are different from you and me.
—F. Scott Fitzgerald

Many wealthy people are different, plain and simple. They think differently than do others. They pay great attention to the relationships they have with others, while many who aren't wealthy will tend to compare themselves to others. The wealthy tend to focus on the value of something—what it can do for them, what it can help them accomplish—while most others focus solely on its cost.

Wealthy people talk mostly about ideas while others talk mostly about people. The wealthy have one eye constantly on the future and the other on the present, while others are fixated on the present and are still stuck in the past and negatively influenced by it.

For the truly wealthy, money is a tool, a way to achieve an end, while others have determined that it is an end in itself. And the truly wealthy focus more on the return they expect rather than the cost of what they invest their time and money in. And that includes their relationships as well as their money.

You'll find that many of the wealthy rely on the advice of financial advisors because they've learned the value of outside, objective advice—another pair of eyes focusing on their ideas, goals, and financial philosophies. They want advice from people whose financial and ethical responsibilities are to them, not to anyone else.

This is also because the wealthy know the risks they can take when they follow their own emotions; they're as prone to do that as anyone else is, but the difference is that they are conscious of that and recognize the value of levelheadedness especially when they suspect they might not be cool, calm, and collected themselves.

What they value the most is a plan and a relationship with a financial advisor, a coach who plays a stabilizing role for them in good times and bad, on offense as well as defense. They want a relationship with a coach who will help them temper their euphoria over big gains as well as their worries about downturns in the market and their emotional urge to pull out of the market and park their funds in a money market account.

The successful wealthy aren't easily swayed by other people's opinions or the newest investment fad, strategy, or product. They realize the necessity of asking themselves if any financial changes they're contemplating would be a deviation from their plans, whether they'd be getting top-heavy in this or that area of investing, and what the tax consequences would be not only for that year but also for ten years down the road. They've developed their instincts to look at the broad and long-term picture and ignore the "noise" of a sudden dip in this or that market.

Some might say that having such an attitude is easy when you're wealthy, but I have a different take on that. I say that many of the wealthy had that attitude to begin with, and that's why they're wealthy today.

In the introduction, I mentioned how important it was for us to assess our attitudes toward money— is acquiring it a goal in itself or a way of achieving a goal beyond it? In my experience with wealthy people, and I have known a good number of them, the "happy" wealthy as I call them, are those who consider money as a means to an end—the happiness they experience when they focus on their relationships and figure out ways of increasing their and others' happiness by using their money as a tool to achieve that. They want to manage their money well because they consider themselves to be stewards rather than owners of what they have. They want to make sure that it does for their families—their spouses, sons and daughters, grandchildren, and others—what it has done for them. Again, they place great importance on their relationships, and they want to ensure, not simply insure, their happiness.

There's another personality trait I've seen in the wealthy that I don't see as frequently as others, and it's an important one—they delegate. This is what I mean by that. So many of us have a DIY mentality— we've learned how to change oil in our cars, paint a room, sew, do some carpentry, and so on. That "I can do it myself and for a lot less" attitude is ingrained in us; it's part of the American spirit of independence.

But think about tasks for which the ante is upped—maybe rewiring a house, rebuilding an engine, installing a new bathroom, or getting the air conditioner going again. In such cases, we're more prone to seek out a pro to handle that even if we look at the bill later and bemoan the cost.

And let's up the ante a little more here. When it comes to needing a root canal or an appendectomy, there's no question that we all value expertise more than money and will seek it out without hesitation.

There's a hierarchy to the tasks we face, and it's most clearly seen in the consequences of making a mistake that could turn out to be costly in terms of dollars, time, health, and worry. At the higher end of this spectrum, we recognize the fact that we should look for expert advice, respect it, and follow it.

That's what drives the wealthy to seek out financial advice. They know that in spite of their wealth (and maybe because of their concern for it), the pros can handle it better than they can. They know there's a lot more at stake than a quick killing in the stock market or getting in on the "ground floor" of a new industry or the latest craze.

It's not that they're risk adverse; some of them have learned to determine the risk level they can tolerate and stick with it. It's that they know themselves well enough to be wary of their emotions, and they seek professional, outside advice when it comes to dentistry and surgery of course but also when it comes to money. They leave such matters to others who have devoted years to studying the wide array of investment opportunities out there, and they keep on doing what they do best. The wealthy think differently. That's usually the way they have achieved, maintained, and grown their wealth.

By the way, they also have a different attitude toward the concept of time—they value it greatly. This is why most of them don't want to do anything themselves unless it's in area of their unique strengths and they're confident they can handle it. Dan Sullivan, my business coach, calls this our "unique ability."

Your unique abilities are the areas in your life where you can have the maximum impact on others and therefor your maximum leverage in the world. Wealthy (and highly productive people in general) tend to delegate almost everything they can in their lives so they can focus on those specific areas where they can produce the greatest impact. They have their abilities and unique areas of competence, and they also recognize that others—car mechanics, surgeons, roofers, lawyers, pastry chefs, you name it—have their areas of expertise as well, so they rely on them while they stick to whatever it is they do the best that has the greatest impact on their and others' lives. They don't want to try to accomplish anything that isn't covered by one of their own abilities; they delegate those tasks to people, and they then develop lasting relationships with them.

CHAPTER 2

YOUR MONEY PHILOSOPHY

Whether you think you can or you can't either way you are right.

– HENRY FORD

E veryone has a money philosophy. Did you know that? Do you know what yours is? I think with just a bit of cogitation, you could arrive at a good explanation of what yours is even if you haven't considered the matter up until now.

Some people have a healthy philosophy about money while others have one that is bad, even toxic. I used to have what I now see was a bad philosophy of money. Back in the late '90s and early '00s, I started doing well as a financial advisor. I'd gotten my feet on the ground, my list of clients was growing, and I was achieving success for them and myself. I'd even hired two people to help me out. I was with a firm in which others in my same position used the staffers there as back-office help, but I was doing well enough that I could hire those two just for myself. I simply needed the help to keep up, and I chose to get it.

But something funny started happening; I was stymied for an explanation for it. I'd achieve a rung on my success ladder, but then, things would go stale for a few months or longer—as much as a year. I wasn't able to sustain my former level of progress, and I'd even slip back at times in terms of business.

Fortunately for me, I had a Harvard-trained psychologist for a business coach. I had many conversations with him about my hitting my head on some sort of ceiling, and he helped me figure out what was holding me back from continuing my trajectory in my profession.

Through a number of question-and-answer sessions, he helped me realize I actually felt guilty about my success. I felt bad—not just uneasy—about earning more than my father ever had. I came to understand that after I told him about my background and my family. My parents were missionaries when I was young. When I was seven, we moved back to the States from the Caribbean, and we had literally nothing. My father took a job as a janitor at night in addition to a day job. You can imagine how tight money was for a family of five with no savings or a big income. I look back on it now and realize we were better off than many—we always had the necessities and not just those—but my folks had to look after every dollar, and I picked up on that attitude. As I'll relate in chapter 5, that had had a long-lasting impact on me and my attitude about money.

But getting back to my coach. At that point in our conversations, I was relating just some of the details about my past rather than my feelings about them. But it began to dawn on him that I could have had a complex about the possibility I'd end up exceeding my father tremendously in terms of income and thus supposedly success. I listened to him. He made sense. Funny thing was how quickly I realized he was correct.

My coach came up with a workaround—a way out of that mental situation for me. He encouraged me to call my father, tell him about my situation and feelings, and simply ask his permission to succeed. I did that even though I couldn't imagine it would help me overcome my seemingly self-imposed hurdles.

"Dad, is it okay if I earn more money than you did in your working years?" I finally asked him.

"Of course that's okay!" he responded. "I'd feel very proud if you did, son."

Strange as it sounds, that solved my problem. I felt relieved of any guilt concerning out-earning my dad because I realized he'd be proud of me if I did. The last thing he'd ever want to do, I had discovered, was to hold back any of his sons or daughters from succeeding wherever they may, and he certainly didn't want them to hold themselves back out of some sense of loyalty to or respect of him.

In hindsight, that's exactly what I would have expected him to say. That's for sure what I'd tell any of my sons and daughters. But back then, my money philosophy was not only a negative, it was also a buried negative in that I simply wasn't aware of it. No surprise at all that such subconscious thoughts were sabotaging all the work I was doing consciously and dragging me down and back. I hadn't been aware of how I felt; I had just felt the way I did and hadn't worried about why.

Others could have money philosophies that are affected by their social or political views—they could consciously or unconsciously resent those who were much richer than they were and not want to be in that position, or they could feel negatively toward those who are poor and simply feel the poor should blame themselves for the positions they are in. They could feel that their children were entitled to attend the best colleges they could get into regardless of the cost, regardless of what effect that would have on their retirement. That's a good example of a money philosophy that involves putting the welfare of others above your own. I'm not saying it's necessarily good or bad; I'm just saying it's a money philosophy that could have a big effect on someone if not now, then down the road. And that's why they should strive to uncover and understand their philosophy of money.

I specialize in financial planning for those in or near retirement, and I've had clients who were hurting a lot financially because they'd sacrificed so much to send their children to expensive, private, college-prep schools and then on to Ivy League schools. They didn't even consider less-expensive schools that would have allowed them to strike a balance between their desire to give their children a good education and what they'd need in retirement. I don't mean this to sound at all flippant, but some

folks who go this route end up living out their re-
tirements with their well-educated sons and daughters—not the best of circumstances for either party.

My current executive coach, Dan Sullivan, deals
with these money philosophies as well. He's met
people who feel there's some kind of honor in living lives of poverty, that there's a nobility in living
in misery, that they don't deserve to be successful.
The question, "Just who does he think he is?" gets
turned around to "Just who do I think I am?" When
he mentioned that to me, it reinforced what I had
learned about myself earlier.

My personal experience and my experiences with
my clients have driven home the point to me that we
all have money philosophies even though they can
be hidden from our conscious thoughts. It can take
definite effort on our part to determine what our individual philosophies are, and it can take even more
effort if their roots are in our pasts, our feelings, our
intuitions, and our ways of viewing life. Those can
be tough things to put into words if we haven't done

that already. We just feel the way we do, and we accept our feelings and attitudes as givens. But when those feelings clash with our conscious thoughts about money ("Of course I'd love to be wealthy!"), we can feel a dissonance, an unease, a nagging that's hard to ignore.

As a way to start uncovering your feelings—not your everyday thoughts—about money, think about when you were growing up. Were you well off or poor? It takes more than answering that off the top of your head. We've all read about people who said they'd grown up poor but didn't realize that because all the others on their blocks were in the same or similar financial situations and their parents, friends, and neighbors were caring and loving, and that made things so much easier.

On the other hand, some people grew up thinking they were poor because their parents had never bought them a Sting-Ray bike or a Wilson A-2000 baseball glove for a birthday present. They didn't realize then that big families couldn't easily spring for the hearts' desires of every child or that their parents had made a conscious decision to make sure they didn't grow up spoiled or feeling they were entitled to all their whims and desires. They can realize that now, but subconsciously, they could still be carrying around feelings of unfulfilled wants.

Other people might remember a father working two jobs and not being home a lot so the mother could focus on raising the family and managing the household. That could create ambivalent feelings about money. Some people were taught that the establishment was out to get them so they should get theirs while they could, and others might have been taught that those with government jobs did as little as possible and still expected to collect their paychecks every week.

Some people were totally oblivious to what their grade-school classmates wore and cannot remember to this day who wore the latest styles and who got by with patched hand-me-downs. And others were very conscious of what they wore and judged others as living up to their standards of clothing or falling way short of them. Those are feelings they can unconsciously carry around with them for years and affect their attitude toward money or its lack.

Your experiences can affect how you feel about money (and *feel* is the important word here), but so can your personality. It, of course, will be affected by your past, but your particular personality is the sum of so many factors. Are you a risk taker? Do you live day by day, or do you meticulously plan for today and tomorrow and next month and year as well?

The way you view the world can come into play here as well. Some of us focus on the scarcity apparent in some parts of the world while others can't imagine ever being in want of anything. Some think that if they acquire something, that means someone will have to do without—a zero-sum game—while others imagine that there's more than enough to go around based on the progress we've made, our innate ingenuity, and technology that will continually improve and make life better and more fair worldwide.

Some people's mind-set is that successful people gained whatever they have through hard work and admire them for that, while others assume (or sure hope to learn) that their success was due to underhandedness, or luck, or a great-uncle who got clean away with a bundle back in the day by one nefarious scheme or another.

What charities you donate to and how much you give will also be an indication of your philosophy of money. Some focus on helping the destitute, while others are more drawn to support bootstrap programs that assist ambitious people wherever they are. People can rationalize their charitable giving or lack of it, but I think the attitude precedes and thus directs the rationalization and the giving.

Our philosophies about money take on an even greater importance when we marry and start families. It's common for marriages to take place between two people with different attitudes about money, and if that's the case with you and your spouse, I'll bet you have plenty of stories about that. Consider also what you're indirectly teaching your children about money; realize that they could be picking up some very different and confusing signals from you and your spouse. That in itself is a good reason to think about your philosophy of money all the way to the point that you could easily explain it to others if you ever felt the need to and not have nagging doubts or internal dissonance about your view.

I offer you a little quiz here. There are no rights or wrongs here, simply questions you can answer from your gut that will start you down the road to determining what your philosophy of money is. Circle 1 if you "strongly disagree" up to 5, "strongly agree."

My spouse and I agree on major purchases (houses, car, etc.)

1   2   3   4   5

My spouse and I agree on minor purchases (nights out, new lawnmower, gifts).

    1   2   3   4   5

I grew up in a financially secure family.

    1   2   3   4   5

I have a hard time determining what I should do with a refund, a gift of money, a $20 I find in my jeans, or other such minor "windfalls."

    1   2   3   4   5

I consistently balance my "checkbook" to the penny.

    1   2   3   4   5

I buy lottery tickets and fantasize about winning.

    1   2   3   4   5

I would have no problem figuring out what to do with a $100,000 inheritance.

    1   2   3   4   5

I'm willing to donate to a charity a neighbor or friend might recommend to me.

    1   2   3   4   5

I enjoy reading about what the wealthy do with their money just for fun.

    1   2   3   4   5

I don't begrudge the wealthy being in the situation they're in.

    1   2   3   4   5

I worry about having enough money to last me through retirement.

    1   2   3   4   5

I feel my spouse will have enough to live on after I'm gone.

1   2   3   4   5

I want to leave as big a pile of money to my sons and daughters as I can.

1   2   3   4   5

I have no sympathy for those who declare bankruptcy.

1   2   3   4   5

I compare my siblings', friends', and neighbors' financial success to my own.

1   2   3   4   5

I tend to go overboard when it comes to buying gifts for others.

1   2   3   4   5

I find myself trying to guess other peoples' incomes.

1   2   3   4   5

I'm not worried about my present financial situation.

1   2   3   4   5

I'm often reluctant to "treat" myself to a gift.

1   2   3   4   5

This is just a start. I'm guessing that these questions have prompted you to ask and answer other questions the above have raised. I encourage you to answer these questions and others as they come up in the same way, but dig a tad deeper—answer the implied follow-up question—Why?

It's not so much the number of dollars we have but how we feel about them that's critical in bringing our hearts and minds to an agreement on the matter. But achieving that accord is well worth the effort in that it will help us frame all our future financial questions and we'll be on more-solid ground with our answers and the financial plans we craft based on them.

CHAPTER 3

THE CROWD IS USUALLY WRONG

It is better to walk alone than with a crowd going in the wrong direction.

– DIANE GRANT

At the time of this writing, I have one in college and two who have graduated from college. I have witnessed their education from kindergarten on up all these years, and that has prompted me to reflect on my own education and its principles from a perspective I didn't have when I was being educated.

I now look on the educational process as one of assimilation, of learning how to conform. Kids enter the educational system as products of their families with rough edges and all. As they progress through the educational system, those rough edges get filed off, the holes get filled in and sanded, and they learn what's considered appropriate and inappropriate as far as behavior is concerned. They develop outlooks and attitudes that align with those of their teachers, and by trial and error (and a bunch of prompting), they pick up on how to function with their peers and adults in ways that cause little friction. Out come "products" that pretty well conform to each other and the system that was responsible for creating them.

Education is indeed a sort of manufacturing model—raw materials go in, and some years later, finished products come out. Society encourages those of us who conform to its standards and norms and rejects those of us who are a little different.

I'm a contrarian in this regard, and I believe I have good reason to be that way. Conjure up the images of three people you admire, three who stick out in your mind as exemplars of remarkable people, three who stand far above others in your estimation. I'll bet they weren't or aren't conformists. I'll bet they were or are distinct from so many others.

Many will think of Mother Teresa, Steve Jobs, Michael Jordan, Stephen Hawking, John F. Kennedy, and Ronald Reagan just for a handful of examples. Ask a hundred people and you'd probably end up with a bunch of duplicate names, but you'll also come across many singletons who you'd probably agree were at least worthy of mention. And the vast majority if not all would be nonconformists, people who stuck out for a variety of reasons, people who were unique.

Why do we admire such people? My strong feeling is that it's because they lived lives so different from those their contemporaries lived and did so based on personal choice, not their circumstances that in many cases they had to overcome. They stood out for their outlooks and accomplishments that few of their peers could match or even dared try to match.

I can't understand exactly why conformists admire nonconformists; it's a psychological question I'm not equipped to answer, but I've seen it frequently in myself and others. Who doesn't want to rub at least psychological shoulders with the greats and daydream about being in their shoes? That attitude comes into play in the investment world, where those who take nonconformist stances succeed much more frequently than do those who follow the crowd out of habit, inertia, or fear. It's because the nonconformists have learned that the crowd is usually wrong, that its behavior is very frequently wrong and counterproductive as well.

This concept has been the subject of numerous studies that tried to answer the question, What do nonconformists know and then do that puts them so far ahead of the pack? Discover the answer, bottle it, and it would market itself; it would be a gold mine.

The majority at best is mediocre, and usually, it's worse than that. But to go against the grain, the herd, whatever you want to call it, requires a psychological fortitude few have, and that's the case especially during downturns in the market.

This is why you'll read about a certain mutual fund doing great one year but those who invested in it doing poorly that same year. Let me explain. The reason for the difference is not the fees involved but the investors' behavior, and that can be influenced by the crowd. They can become fearful at certain news and withdraw from a mutual fund that has gone down. A loss. They reinvest in the fund after it's gone up. Not quite the same as a loss but a definite forgone opportunity for a gain.

They get edgy again later in the year when the mutual fund falls because the broader market has, and they pull out again. They pull out after they've lost, and they don't get back in until the market goes up; they were following the herd instinct character-ized by fear and greed, two major obstacles when it comes to investing. Their behavior with their invest-ments, not their investments themselves, causes the problem, and that can be costly.

Do we really think there's safety in numbers? Maybe antelopes, gazelles, and buffalo do, but we shouldn't. And that's particularly the case when it comes to investments. John Templeton said, "If you want to have better performance than the crowd, you must do things differently than the crowd."

DALBAR, a financial services market research firm, publishes annual studies of investor returns, and it's been doing that for over twenty years. They call it quantitative analysis of investor behavior (QAIB), and it "examines the returns that investors actually realize and the behaviors that produce those returns."[1] Here's a bit more from its site.

QAIB has been measuring the effects of investor decisions to buy, sell and switch into and out of mutual

1   www.dalbar.com/ProductsServices/AdvisorSolutions/QAIB/tabid/214/Default.aspx

funds over both short- and long-term time frames. The results consistently show that the average investor earns less—in many cases, much less—than mutual fund performance reports would suggest.

From 1994 to 2013, the S&P 500's total annualized return was 9.22 per cent. During that time, the average equity mutual fund investor earned 5.02 per cent. So the average investor has underperformed the index by 4.2 per cent per year. That is a huge difference ... The *only* possible explanation is that equity investors on average buy or sell their funds at the wrong time. And this is a consequence of a very short holding time period: on average, the average equity mutual fund investor kept his shares for 3.33 years. That is a third of a typical business cycle.[2]

These numbers were true as of 2013, and of course they change from year to year, but the principle has unfortunately been consistent. Every year tells the same story: investors in motion lose out on what they could have gained if their behavior had been consistent. They bail after losses and don't re-enter the market until it rebounds, but then they've suffered a loss and completely missed out on that

2   http://montrealgazette.com/business/local-business/personal-finance/why-most-investors-dont-come-close-to-earning-average-returns.

rebound. They're boxers who protect their head after they've taken a blow there and leave their stomachs unprotected and subject to a punch there. They then cover their stomachs and take a right hook to the cranium ad infinitum. They allow their emotions to override what they in all likelihood started with—a buy-and-hold strategy.

"At no point in time have average investors remained invested for a sufficiently long enough period to derive the benefits of a long-term investment strategy," DALBAR wrote in its 2011 investor behavior analysis, and nothing's changed since then.

I encourage my clients to turn off CNBC and such channels that rely heavily on soundbites; they're more for entertainment than news. No network wants to be scooped by another, so they all rush to broadcast the latest financial scare, and never mind if it turns out to be just that—a scare.

DALBAR has data to back up its claim that those investors who put their money into stocks and bonds—a balanced portfolio—are somewhat more successful. They tend to hold onto their investments longer, and a big reason for that is because they take into consideration the whole pie and refuse to focus on any particular slice. As well, they don't expect their balanced portfolios to zoom in value; they've invested the way they have because they want diversification so they won't experience drastic dips. That comes at the price of not enjoying big jumps to their fullest, but they're psychologically prepared for that because they have a much longer investment horizon in mind.

I like to say that their expectations are appropriate. They look at the aggregate and ignore the particulars; that's why they don't worry about this or that stock or bond in their portfolios underperforming the market because they're pretty sure that others will match or even outperform the market and make up for the slacker.

I've had clients with twenty, thirty different investments who would zero in and focus solely on the two or three that were doing really poorly or very well. "Can we dump these and invest in those?" They fall prey to what's known as recency bias, the idea that whatever's taking place at the time will likely keep taking place in the future. I'm subject to that bias just as much as anyone else is; it's an emotional response, and it's hard for our minds to override our emotions. The difference is that certain people, and I include many of the wealthy in this number, have the ability to recognize it when it rears its head and resist it.

As a financial advisor, I take the role of a coach and stress to our clients that no one would ever need a portfolio and the balancing effect it can have on investments if he or she was sure of what stocks were going to do well and which would flounder in the coming year. There's no crystal ball, and those who realize that have a much better chance of having their dreams fulfilled rather than dashed.

Michael Jordan, Mother Teresa, Steve Jobs, and others like them didn't achieve what they did by following the crowd; quite the opposite. I want everyone, not just my clients, to do what amounts to frank self-analysis and discover their personal propensity to follow the crowd. What the crowd does is considered common wisdom, but in my mind, it doesn't deserve the name *wisdom*. Sometimes, you have to be able to row upstream and ignore all those going with the flow.

CHAPTER 4

TIME: YOUR MOST VALUABLE COMMODITY

*Time is more valuable than money. You can get
more money, but you cannot get more time.*

– JIM ROHN

I want to dig into a concept that I've found not only fascinating but also very important, and it applies to everyone—trading time for money or trading money for time. Let me explain the distinction I want to make, and it's a critical one. Time is the most valuable commodity we all have. Money may come in second—a close second—but it will never be as important as time—yours, mine, and everyone's.

I think you'll find that many people always have their eyes out for bargains whether they involve food, clothes, cars, cell phones, and so on. Many folks read the ads, go online, and scout out in many other ways the best buys and feel a certain amount of satisfaction when they think they've scored a bargain.

But let's analyze that thinking and what it can result in. Let's say the store closest to you is selling your favorite water for $5 a case—good stuff that has become your favorite. But then you happen to read an ad put out by a store across town that's offering the same product for $3.50, and you come up with some justification to go to that second store so you can snag the savings on the water. You might decide to make the trip more worthwhile by getting other things there, but if they're simply impulse purchases—things you could have done without with no problem—delete their cost from the $1.50 you expect to save.

So you spend twenty minutes going there and twenty minutes coming back; you just spent forty minutes of your life to save $1.50. What you're saying in essence is that your time is worth $2.25 an hour not counting the extra gas. That's an example of spending time to save money, and you can see how that can—not in all such instances, but it can—cost you something that's more valuable than money.

Most wealthy people would handle such a situation this way. They'd realize the false economy in driving across town to save that $1.50, and they'd even spring for a delivery service for all their shopping. Depending on what they bought in total, the delivery charge could drive the price of that case of water up an extra buck spread out over the other purchases, but they saved not only the forty minutes driving across town but also the time they would have spent going to and shopping in the first place.

I'm sure you know people who grew up in families that were not well to do or even what you'd call poor; that could have been your situation as well.

But in those families, perhaps due to the number of children, every dollar, every dime, every nickel held a value greater for them than it did for many others' families. Maybe they saw their parents being frugal at every turn, and I'm willing to bet that rubbed off on them. That was my case, and it was the case with my wife.

Today, they might hesitate even contemplating a vacation to somewhere they've always wanted to go or to buy a new car. I'm willing to bet that guilt factors into their thinking; they might feel they're going against their upbringing even though they're no longer in the same financial situation their parents and siblings were. That was my case as I mention in chapter 6. Simply put, their upbringing can lead them to value money more than time because that attitude was ingrained in them when they were very young, was reinforced as the years went on, and became a habit—unconscious and unquestioned behavior.

I heard a story about someone who grew up in a family like that. His family wasn't poor, but it was big—eight children—which can often have the same effect. He knew he'd have to wait in line for his needs to be fulfilled because his brothers and sisters had needs too.

One day, the water heater broke down. He convinced his dad to drive to Sears and buy one and bring it back in the family station wagon, which was a secondhand car. He and his dad lugged it down to the basement, and the boy figured out how to drain the old water heater, disconnect the gas line, and monkey-wrench the cold-water pipe going in and the hot-water pipe coming out. The young man installed the water heater himself after a trip or two to the hardware store. He knew even then why he was driven to do that—plumbers were expensive. He valued the money his family saved more than the time he spent hooking up the water and gas line. All that at age sixteen.

He was surprised that his father had let him tackle such a project, but years later, he decided his father had done that because he had the same attitude about money versus time and had been willing to let his son handle such a task to save the bucks. He then realized he had inherited in a sense that attitude from his father. He now hires plumbers of course.

I know someone who also grew up in a not poor but certainly not wealthy family. She handled chores, babysitting, and cooking duties as most kids do, but she absorbed a lesson—getting others to handle such chores cost money.

Years later, she and her husband were doing very well. Though she was the mother of four, she was reluctant to hire a housekeeper even for just one day a week. She innately felt that she was the one who had to handle the chores; that's how she had been raised. So squiring the kids to this or that volleyball or baseball practice, shopping, cooking, walking the dog—on and on—fell to her. Some evenings, she'd end up exhausted and out of time, but that was the price she was willing to pay to save her family some money.

On the other hand, most wealthy people would rather trade their money for time because they realize they can get more money but they can never get more time. I know a very successful businessman whose company purchased a private jet. There's no way you can save money by buying a private jet rather than flying commercial; you don't have to be an accountant to figure that one out. But he wasn't interested in saving money. He was interested in saving time.

He was a veteran traveler by that time who had spent hours and hours at airports waiting for flights and scrambling for alternate flights after they would be cancelled due to bad weather and so on. He did some calculations, and he determined that he'd be able to spend no less than seventy-two more nights with his family each year if he bought that jet and could take control his own flight schedules.

Seventy-two more nights with his family? They money he spent bought him invaluable time with his family. He never regretted trading money for time.

Not all of us can buy a jet to save ourselves time, but we certainly can find ways to avoid wasting our time driving across town to save a $1.50 on a case of water. It's a matter of attitude, not dollars. It's a matter of deciding to save time whenever and wherever we can even if it's at the expense of money.

Some people will spend a great deal of their time trying to earn and save money, and they obsess over the financial benchmarks they set for themselves. What they fail to realize, however, is how much more valuable their time is than the money they earn and save.

How we decide to use our time will depend on how much we value it. And that will have a great effect on how we create our financial future.

What's it worth to you to spend time the way you want?

CHAPTER 5

EVERYONE HAS A STORY

When you're searching the horizon when your eyes look back. When you're standing in the moment every life has a soundtrack.

— BRETT ELDREDGE

E veryone has a story. And everyone's story is personal. We can share similarities with all kinds of people, but the total mix of what makes us up makes us unique.

Take me, for instance. My father was a minister; my parents were missionaries in the Caribbean, where I grew up until age seven, when we moved to

Minneapolis. Everything my family owned fit in a few steamer trunks and suitcases—no moving van necessary.

My father got busy supporting our family. He worked as a janitor cleaning offices at night, and he showed films for the Billy Graham Association in churches in Minnesota and four surrounding states.

Things became more financially stable for us when he developed a career in the publishing industry, and he started earning enough for us to buy nice cars and take vacations, so we had some of what I consider luxuries, and we enjoyed them. However, we all learned to value what we had.

I have to say that we weren't poor; we were in the middle class, and I can't remember ever lacking the necessities. My siblings and I attended private Christian schools for some of our childhood rather than public schools, and that involved paying tuition that wouldn't have been necessary had we attended public schools, but it was what my parents wanted and valued, so they made sure it happened.

All in all, I'd say I was brought up to be financially conservative; I learned to value a buck—those I earned and those I spent—because my family had to watch all of them that came in and went out.

Wendy, my wife, was one of four children. Her father worked in sales for a subsidiary of Eastman Kodak in Buffalo, so her family was middle class as well. Her mother was a stay-at-home mom, and she actually lives in the house in which Wendy had grown up. Wendy didn't lack the necessities of life, but she didn't get the keys to a new Mustang as a high school graduation gift either if you know what I mean.

Wendy and I married in 1987, and we bought a condo. The $84,000 mortgage that entailed was my first big lesson in economics in a much broader sense; it was the beginning of my financial education. Wendy and I learned how mortgages worked— our initial monthly payments of course went mostly toward the interest and not that much toward the principal at the beginning and for a long time after that. We realized it would be a matter of time before the checks we sent in monthly would go more toward the principal than the interest, but we realized that was the price we'd have to pay to live how and where we wanted and to gain some equity in our home; we certainly looked forward to that.

We also started realizing how money worked, or rather, how our money—no matter how much we were pulling in—should be working for us. We were managing our finances well enough that when an insurance salesman suggested we buy life insurance to cover our liabilities and each other, I started looking at insurance payments not as money down the drain but as a necessary financial defense. All we could afford at the time was term life insurance, but I made sure to get what we needed at that particular time in our financial lives.

I wanted to make sure that if I died, Wendy would receive $150,000 to pay off our place and give her enough so that she could resettle into her new life. We took out a $100,000 policy on Wendy for much the same reason, but it was less because my income was higher.

I always recommend to my clients that they buy the amount of life insurance they need to cover their liabilities, and their liabilities include what incomes their families are relying on and what new expenses—childcare, retraining for a new job or career—those they might leave behind would require. I tell my clients that whether they buy term or whole life insurance can be decided by other issues—the important thing was to have insurance and a sufficient amount of it.

Wendy and I realized the importance of ensuring our lifestyle to put it in very basic terms. Our goal at that point was to have enough insurance to cover our liabilities and one or two years of income for the survivor. We knew that having children would demand higher amounts of life insurance, so we were prepared for that.

On top of that, as soon as I could, I took out disability insurance because I wanted to protect

Wendy in the event I'd become incapacitated and unable to earn a living. I did so for exactly the same reasons we had taken out life insurance policies.

She and I moved to Florida shortly after we had our first child. I'd been in the music and entertainment industry, and I continued in that down in Florida. But soon enough, I decided I wanted a different career, something that would provide all of us more financial security. So in 1989, I became a licensed stockbroker in Florida.

Sometime later, we moved back to Connecticut because we thought it would be a better place to raise a family and that I'd find better opportunities in the financial services industry there. We upped my life insurance to $300,000 and Wendy's to $200,000 because at that point, we wanted to cover living expenses for three to five years as well as our liabilities, and we also wanted to make sure our children's education would be covered. Our financial situation had changed, and I wanted our financial protection to change with that. Of course, we never considered our children to be liabilities—write-offs of course—but you get my point; they were loved ones Wendy and I wanted to protect and provide for in case either of us died.

And then when I was thirty-two, we bought a nicehouse in Manchester, Connecticut, with of course a larger mortgage, and that prompted me to increase my life insurance again; I upped it to $500,000 to cover the mortgage and provide two or three years of income for Wendy and our children. And by that time, my income had increased substantially, so I definitely wanted to make sure that as our financial state improved, our financial plans would keep pace with it.

At the same time, we started saving for retirement. In hindsight, I'm sure glad we had the foresight to do that. We've all heard sad stories of people getting so caught up in their day-to-day struggles that they end up age fifty-eight, seven or eight years from when they'd planned to retire, and realize they don't have enough to supplement the Social Security they're expecting and won't be able to live the lifestyle they've long since become accustomed to.

My point here is that no matter who you are and no matter how much you're earning, your financial plan and insurance protection should grow as your income grows and that your financial horizon should increase all the way to retirement. And the sooner you start focusing on retirement, the better.

Do you remember how you felt when you bought your first car? Got married? Closed on your first condo or home? Had your first child? Your second? On each of those occasions, I felt a mixed bag of emotions—pride and a sense of accomplishment mixed with a dash of apprehension and doubt and a side order of trepidation. My responsibilities were growing with each achievement, each milestone, and I'd ask myself, *Just how am I going to pull this off?* Men in particular tend to mask such feelings, but believe me, they're there.

And our family had grown. Brandon was born in 1990, followed by Michael in 1995, Joel in 1997, and

Noah in 1999. Wendy was a stay-at-home mom, but staying at home with children as anyone with children knows is the farthest thing from sitting back and watching the soaps and drinking iced tea.

Hers was a demanding task for many years; she rode herd over four children whose needs varied with their ages and changed over time for them individually. Fortunately, my income more than covered our expenses, but what she was doing was more like a job and a half or even two. Our thinking was that if she died, I'd incur child-care costs and a lot of them, so we wanted to insure her life to cover that. Her work at home had a tremendous value that neither of us ever underestimated.

Our lives were getting generally more expensive, but fortunately, my income was more than keeping pace with that. Besides putting as much as I could into a 401(k), we increased our life insurance to reflect my growing income and my family's reliance on it. At that point, I'm happy to say my income was six figures. If I died, I didn't want Wendy to have to find a job outside the home; I wanted to make sure she could afford to concentrate on raising our children and do so in a way that wasn't that much financially different from the life we had together.

All this prompted me to increase my life insurance to $1 million, and I increased my disability insurance so in the event of an accident or hospitalization, I'd still bring in $5,000 a month. Those figures sound drastic as they did to us at the time, but they were based on some simple calculations. At that time, I wanted to expand the number of years Wendy and our boys would be covered particularly and especially with college coming up; I wanted to have enough for her and the boys to live on for ten years. If your income is $100,000, you'll need $1 million to do that, so that's what we did.

And the increased disability insurance I took out was for much the same reason; my inability to work for whatever reason would put my family in dire financial straits, and life insurance wouldn't cover that.

But beware of a particular catch with disability insurance—insurance companies won't give you disability insurance that will cover your total income; their thinking is that if all your income were covered, you'd have little incentive to get back to work. So they'll be willing to write disability policies that top out at about 60 to 65 percent of your income maximum. My advice to you is to get as much disability insurance as you can; it probably won't be all you need, but look at it this way—it's that much more than you and your family would have if you weren't receiving it.

As I mentioned before, don't agonize over whether to buy term or whole-life insurance. The most important thing is to have the right amount of life insurance—remember my ten-year's worth of income suggestion—and increase it consistently as your needs grow. By consistently, I don't mean every year; I mean when whatever you're trying to insure—your growing responsibilities, your increasing income, and the reliance your family has on that—requires greater coverage.

When I reached my forties, my family and I were comfortable enough that I started saving 10 to 20 percent of my income. That came at an expense of course—it meant not "buying up" in the housing market every six or seven years, or going on long family vacations all over Europe, or trading in cars every two or three years. But I was willing to do so because of the way I'd grown up—my frugal nature would prompt my brain to ask me, *Do you really need this? You know you should save it, invest it, and let it grow.* And Wendy's thoughts were the same based on her upbringing. She and I had the same money philosophy coursing through our veins. And besides, we had four boys we wanted to put through college.

Here's the rule that I stress: start saving 15 percent of your income when you're in your thirties; if you put it in mutual funds instead of trying to pick stocks or time the market, based on historical models, you'll be in good shape when you turn sixty-five. And as your income grows, so should the percentage of it that you save. You might start out saving just 5 percent, and then you up that to 10 percent, but don't stop there. Get to the point that you can save 15 and even 20 percent by living conservatively—don't begrudge every penny you spend; have fun and enjoy life with it but only after your savings goals are met. Consider saving the same way you consider your bills; pay them first and then look at what's left.

Of course, I have to put in a disclaimer here: the past doesn't predict the future, so no one can guarantee any particular outcome to any investment plan, and another bust like we went through in '08 and '09 could occur again. But the longer the trajectory of your savings years, the better you'll be able to weather downturns, even drastic ones, without panicking.

Well, our financial planning based on our financial conservatism has worked well for us. All four boys attended or are attending college; we were able to do that because the vacations we took weren't full-blown world tours, we didn't house-hop, and we weren't worried about driving five- or six-year-old cars.

Another disclaimer here, this one about our college expenses: Michael received a full-ride scholarship to the University of Colorado in the Marine ROTC program, so we had minimal costs for him. He recently graduated and was commissioned a second lieutenant. But we were able to cover the others' college expenses.

I'll recommend one thing we did: I had our oldest take out student loans that totaled $20,000 because I wanted him to get a real sense of the bucks involved in a college education; I didn't want him to think he was simply entitled to one or that they occurred by magic. After he graduated, I told him that I'd handle his loans, but you know what? He said he'd pay it off himself. And he is doing just that. I'm proud to think that some of Wendy and me had rubbed off on him.

When another son, who was attending the University of Connecticut, told us that he wanted to upgrade his campus housing the next year, we told him that was fine as long as he was able to come up with some of the money maybe by working on campus or saving more from his summer job. Tough love? No, it was plain old love mixed with a desire to instill in him the same financial consciousness Wendy and I had.

I mentioned this before, but it's critical advice I have for everyone: if you sacrifice your future, your retirement, for the sake of putting your son or daughter through a very expensive school, you might end up spending your retirement years under the roof of a very educated son or daughter. And that would be a situation neither party would want.

I really worry about those whose lifestyles require their spending 100 percent of their incomes. They're not allowing for retirement of course, but also, they're not allowing for financial emergencies—hospital bills, layoffs, and so on. I encourage all my clients to live comfortably but start saving as soon as they can. I tell them to make deposits into their savings accounts, 401(k)s, and so on as if they were bills, and then have fun with what remains.

Keep in mind that if you put off starting a savings plan until you're forty, you'll have to start saving at least 20 percent of your income to simply catch up to where you would have been had you started saving a smaller percentage before that.

Today, Wendy and I are in our midfifties and enjoying upper middle-class lives. We're well off, but we're still saving well over 20 percent of our income and still buying insurance because we want to protect what we have of course, but more important, because Wendy and I simply love our sons; that motivation has always been in the forefront of our financial decisions. Some financial decisions are made for selfish reasons, and I think that's okay. If someone would really get enjoyment out of a bass boat, I'd encourage that person to go ahead and buy it. But I think the best and the most significant decisions are based on love.

I've run across many wealthy people, and it became apparent to me very quickly whether they were happy or miserable. Those whom I call happy were focused on others—their families, their employees, and those who were less fortunate than they were. The unhappy ones were like Scrooge—they were fearful, suspicious, greedy, and unloving.

If we think and act as the happy wealthy do, no matter what our situations in life are, we will be more fulfilled. Our values and obligations will drive our financial decisions. Happiness doesn't come from the money we have but the *attitude* we have toward that money. Its worth lies in its ability to create value in others' lives as well as our own.

I believe that the happy wealthy would act and think the same way they do even if their wealth were to suddenly vanish. That's because they don't equate their sense of self, life, happiness, and love with a bottom-line figure.

Wendy's and my story is very similar to those I hear from clients—it's a mixture of many emotions including fear of loss of course but also hope and love. Our inner values and our sense of responsibility and obligation to each other and our sons have resulted in financial decisions that I can truly say have given us a definite sense of fulfillment in life.

And it just doesn't get better than that.

CHAPTER 6

OUR TEAM PHILOSOPHY

You can do what I cannot do. I can do what you cannot do. Together we can do great things.

— Mother Teresa

Our team at Johnson Brunetti takes a very different approach to financial advising that is in marked contrast to the approaches many other financial advisory firms take— instead of talking to you, we listen to you. The folks at Johnson Brunetti are real people who truly care about hard-working, real families. We have built our firm by instilling a sense of confidence in our clients and their families whether they are just starting out or are approaching their retirement years.

We *listen* to our clients and our potential clients, and we do so intently—it's much more than a nice line; it represents our basic philosophy of financial advising. That's the only way we know how to serve our clients the best. And that's been the reason for our success and our client's success with managing their money for many years now.

Our most important asset as a financial advising company is the trust our clients put in us, so we do everything we can to earn and deserve that trust. They choose us to give them financial advice because they quickly learn that we care about their goals, dreams, and concerns and we provide them a safe space to discuss their wishes for their money. Some may want to leave it to children or grandchildren. Some may want to leave it to a cause they hold close to their hearts. We cherish and honor the relationships we have established with our clients, so we take those relationships very seriously and honor them—no hyperbole there.

We could do what so many other financial advisors do and simply ask our clients for all their financials—stocks, IRAs, tax returns, savings accounts, current and potential earnings, and so on—and then go into the back room, crunch some numbers, and come out with a game plan, but we don't. Such a plan would reflect our thinking but not necessarily that of our clients. We've long since learned that our clients' financials—whether they are relatively simple or complex, whether their bottom lines are relatively small or huge—are just details. They're of course important details, but still, they're just details. We look at those details as our starting point.

What's much more important to us is what our clients have to tell *us*. And when they speak, we're quiet. We want to learn as much as we can about our clients including their dreams, goals, and values, their attitudes toward money, their fears, the unknowns they want cleared up including what they should put aside for college, a vacation home, retirement, and so much more of what I call information that comes from the heart, not from a bank or brokerage statement. The biggest question most people have is, "Will I run out of money in retirement?"

We've listened to people who in some cases were verbalizing their thoughts on their finances for the first time, and some didn't have a clear picture of exactly what their philosophy of money was or what exactly they wanted to accomplish with it right off the bat. But that's okay. We listened as they expressed their thoughts to us. That's because before we can come up with a financial plan based on the details, we first have to really understand our clients and their individual situations.

It's only *after* we at Johnson Brunetti feel we really know someone that we then feel we can craft a financial plan that will match their goals and dreams, quell their worries, and give them a good outline and thus hope for their financial futures.

As a firm, we've long since ruled out inflicting the industry's "jargon" on our clients; throwing around buzzwords rarely impresses anybody, and unfortunately, the financial advising industry is loaded with acronyms—REITs, DAPTs, FLPs, and so many others. We work hard to keep things simple because we've had experience dealing with clients who were just starting down their financial paths and were focusing on their careers, jobs, and professions and didn't have time to dive into the big ocean of financial planning on their own.

But that doesn't mean we take a simplistic approach to financial management. We have all the portfolio-building tools we need to analyze anyone's total financial situation; we will run that person's total financials through all kinds of detailed analyses to come up with a plan for that specific person in his or her specific situation.

While our clients will work primarily with one advisor—their point person at Johnson Brunetti—that advisor has a team backing him or her up. They meet as a team, discuss a client's situation, and collectively decide what's in any one client's best interests. I stress the client's best interests because we're fiduciaries; that means we make decisions based on what is best for our clients, not us or anyone else. Being a fiduciary means we are ethically and legally bound to act and make decisions in that manner.

Our team works together very closely and is actively engaged in the decisions its members recommend regarding each family's financial picture. And then, we present our potential clients with a one-page plan that represents our recommendations. Not a binder stuffed with statistics, bar graphs, charts, formulae, and so on that can easily become overwhelming. Just one page. That page will include what we offer to do for that client after we're sure we understand him or her well enough to have a solid grasp on what that person's wants, fears, needs, and desires are. There are of course lots of backup documents that go with that one page, but most people want to keep things simple.

Our culture is something we fiercely protect here at Johnson Brunetti. Our growing team of 30-plus people have an open-office format that encourages collaboration, communication, and a growth mindset. We care about our team's growth, and you can consistently find someone from any department whether marketing, project managers, our specialists, or our client relationship coordinators involved in learning and growth opportunities to continuously strive to serve you better.

The staff at Johnson Brunetti are actively engaged in our community. We work closely with Make a Wish, The Salvation Army, Veterans, Channel 3 Kids Camp, and Camp Courant. Our team and our clients enjoy being involved in the many events we are honored to be a part of; we're people who also have dreams and hopes. You'll find us to be a lot like you.

We work hard to be thorough in what we do, but we also aim to keep things simple. Because we value your time.

Why do I tell you all this? It's not to impress you. I tell you this so you can judge whether we are a good fit for you. We're not the right firm for everybody, so it's important that you know who we are as you seek a company you will trust.

WA